W9-DGE-417

BEFORE THE DINOSAURS

BEFORE THE DINOSAURS

by Carla Greene

illustrated by Richard Cuffari

THE BOBBS-MERRILL COMPANY, INC.

INDIANAPOLIS   NEW YORK

The author wishes to express her appreciation
to Dr. Edward C. Wilson, Curator of Invertebrate Paleontology,
and Dr. Shelton P. Applegate, Associate Curator of Vertebrate Paleontology,
of the Los Angeles County Museum of Natural History,
for reading the first manuscript and offering valuable suggestions.

The Bobbs-Merrill Company, Inc.
A Subsidiary of Howard W. Sams & Co., Inc.
Publishers Indianapolis Kansas City New York
Text copyright © 1970 by Carla Greene
Illustrations copyright © 1970 by Richard Cuffari
Printed in the United States of America
Library of Congress catalog card number: 70-119376
First printing
Designed by Jack Jaget

Contents

Early Life on Earth

Of course you know about the dinosaurs. You may have read about the giant reptiles. Perhaps you have seen skeletons or reproductions in a museum. Or you may have seen them in movies or on television.

It's hard to take our minds back many millions of years. Yet we know that dinosaurs lived from two hundred million years ago to seventy million years ago. These prehistoric reptiles ruled the earth for more than one hundred million years. Then they disappeared forever.

The history of dinosaurs is indeed an exciting one. It has been told in many books, including this author's HOW TO KNOW DINOSAURS. But do you know the fascinating story of life on earth over the billions of years *before* the dinosaurs? What led up to

7

the existence of these strange creatures—some no larger than a chicken, yet several of them many times larger than any animal living today? How did they come into being?

To find some answers to these questions it is important to know that all living things go through a long, slow process of change which is known as *evolution*. No human being ever lives long enough to observe these tiny changes which take place generation after generation. Over millions of years, animals slowly evolve with new physical characteristics which help them to find food and protect themselves from enemies, thus enabling them to survive better in their surroundings. These continuous improvements sometimes result in an entirely new species. (A species is a group of animals or plants all having the same basic physical characteristics and habits. The individuals of a species mate only with their own kind.) Some species may have lived on from the beginning of recorded time to the present. On the other hand, some species, such as the dinosaurs, have disappeared entirely. No one knows exactly why.

Another thing we must keep in mind is that scientists believe the earth to be *five and one-half billion* years old. The surface of the earth and the climate are constantly changing. For long periods in the past, many parts of the world were covered by seas. At other times, when volcanoes erupted and earthquakes shook the earth, mountains gradually rose from beneath the seas and caused the waters to flow back to their former basins, leaving large surfaces of dry land. As the mountains rose, they carried with them samples of the living things which had existed in the seas. These samples have been preserved in the rocks which form the earth's crust, and are called "fossils."

Finding Fossils

Fossils are the remains of ancient living things which have been preserved in rocks in the earth's crust.

The remains of most dead creatures decay or are destroyed by other animals. However, if an animal sinks to the bottom of a sea, river, or lake and is covered by mud, or if the animal dies in a desert and is quickly covered by the sands of a desert storm, the hard parts of the body gradually become stone-like and remain preserved in rocks.

A fossil may be just a piece of rock containing an imprint of plant life, or it may be a series of burrows or trails made by crawling worms. It may be a complete shell of a sea animal or just the mold of a shell which slowly dissolved and was then replaced by minerals which hardened and duplicated the form of the shell. A fossil may be just the outline of a leaf, or it may be a whole plant or even a whole tree trunk which has hardened and become stone-like. It may be the impression of an animal's feet. Or it may be the actual bones of a beast, reptile, fish, bird, or human.

Scientists from leading museums and universities make expeditions to various parts of the world to hunt for fossils. Fossils may be found wherever a rock formation has been cut into, either by natural forces such as a river cutting through rock to form a ravine or a canyon, or by modern machines cutting through rock for a new highway or digging the foundation for a new building. They may also be found in a stone quarry or in the side of a hill or mountain. They may be found buried in a desert or in a dry riverbed.

One of America's greatest rock piles of fossils is in the Grand Canyon of Arizona. Looking down into the canyon, you can see the great gorge, from four to eighteen miles wide, with ledges of rock towering a mile high on each side.

At the bottom of the canyon, the roaring Colorado River tumbles wildly along, carrying mud and silt which even today is cutting through the earth's crust. It has formed the Grand Canyon, a beautiful and awe-inspiring sight. Here we can actually get a look into the interior of the earth.

Looking closely at the ledges, you will see that they consist of many layers of different kinds of rock. Each of these layers was formed during a definite period representing millions of years in the earth's history. The oldest layer is at the bottom, the next oldest above it, and so on upward to the top layer. Paleontologists (PAY-lee-on-TOL-ojists), the scientists who study ancient life, relate the fossils found in each layer to a certain period of time on earth.

The earliest rocks which contain a sizeable collection of fossils are in the layers of the Paleozoic Era which began about 600 million years ago. While living things existed for many millions of years before that time, they left very little fossil record because these plants and animals were mostly soft-bodied. Thus they were very rarely preserved as fossils.

The Paleozoic Era

600 to 225 million years ago

Although fossils have been found showing that plant or bacteria life existed two billion years ago, they are very scarce. The earliest time in which life was recorded by vast quantities of fossils was the Paleozoic Era. In the early part of that era, the land surfaces were totally barren; there were no plants, insects, or land animals. About 200 million years of the Paleozoic Era passed before life began to appear on land. But a great array of living things existed in the seas which covered much of North America and many other parts of the world.

Scientists divide the Paleozoic Era into six periods, each standing for millions of years and each represented in its own layer of rock in the earth's crust.

13

Beginning with the oldest period, which appears in the bottom layer, the periods are as follows:

The Cambrian Period lasted from approximately 600 million years ago to 515 million years ago.

The Ordovician Period lasted from approximately 515 million years ago to 460 million years ago.

The Silurian Period lasted from approximately 460 million years ago to 405 million years ago.

The Devonian Period lasted from approximately 405 million years ago to 345 million years ago.

The Carboniferous Period lasted from approximately 355 million years ago to 265 million years ago.

The Permian Period lasted from approximately 265 million years ago to 225 million years ago.

The Cambrian Period

600 to 515 million years ago

Let's go back 600 million years to the beginning of the Cambrian Period. We must remember that much of North America and many other parts of the world were covered by oceans and shallow seas. Many primitive plants and animals which had evolved in

15

Pre-Cambrian times now lived in the Cambrian seas.

Among the many kinds of sea plants, the tiny organisms we know as *algae* (AL-jee), which we see as green scum on ponds, were present in abundance. During their lifetime, these plants gathered stony material around them which hardened to become great reefs. Some of these reefs began forming as much as a billion years ago. And some are still being built in warm seas.

Numerous kinds of soft-bodied creatures which we call INVERTEBRATES (in-VER-te-brates), many too frail to have been preserved as fossils, made their homes in the seas. Among the animals which left us a good fossil record were the sponges, corals, and jellyfish.

By far the largest group of fossils found in Cambrian rocks was the *trilobites* (TRY-lobe-ites), crab-like creatures that ruled the seas in middle and later Cambrian times.

PROTOZOANS
single-celled creatures

The name PROTOZOANS (PRO-to-ZO-uns) means "first animals." Most scientists classify them as animals, but some consider these organisms as neither animals nor plants. They therefore place them in a group of their own called *protists*.

This simple form of life existed in the seas long before and throughout the Cambrian Period, and its descendants, known as *foraminifera* (for-am-in-IF-era), or *forams* for short, exist in the seas today.

The body of a foram consists of a single cell. The earliest forams did not have shells, but the modern foram's jelly-like flesh is contained in a shell. To feed,

MODERN FORAM

the soft flesh oozes out of the holes in the shell, reaching out in all directions like grasping feet. These "feet" catch tiny morsels of food and digest them outside of the shell, since the foram has neither a mouth nor a stomach. Most forams are so tiny that their details can be seen only through a microscope.

MODERN SPONGES

SPONGES
a forward step

Did you know that sponges are animals? Of course we are referring to *natural* sponges, not the rubber or synthetic ones you often see nowadays. Natural sponges grow in the sea. They have soft, bouncy flesh

18

full of holes. You can wet a sponge and watch it swell, then you can squeeze all the water out and let it dry.

The primitive sponges that lived in Cambrian seas were not much different from modern ones, except for their shape. They were shaped somewhat like a vase with an opening at the top. Like today's sponges, they were full of holes or "pores," and therefore scientists named them *porifera* (po-RIF-er-uh) or pore-bearers.

The early sponge was still a primitive animal, but it represents a distinct advance over the single-celled protozoans. Instead of just one cell, the sponge had many kinds of cells, and each group of cells performed a particular job. One group formed the skeleton of the sponge (the body that is preserved as a fossil). Another group made whips inside the body that set up a beating motion, drawing water into the holes. Other cells removed tiny bits of food from the water to provide nourishment to the animal. And still others rid the body of wastes, shooting the water out of the opening at the top of the sponge.

Since sponges are soft-bodied animals, you may wonder how they could be preserved as fossils. The fact is that some of the sponges of Cambrian times were soft throughout, whereas others had skeletons of glassy or stony material which became hardened enough to become fossils. (Glassy sponges in a variety of shapes lived through later periods of the Paleozoic Era and on into the present.)

COELENTERATES
another step forward

We must remember that Cambrian times lasted for almost one hundred million years. And during that time, evolution was constantly taking place. One of the important groups that had evolved even before the Cambrian Period were the COELENTERATES (see-LEN-ter-ates)—corals, jellyfish, sea anemones, and some other sea creatures. These were the first animals which had mouths to gather food and stomachs to digest it. They were also the first animals to combine their cells to form tissues. A tissue, consisting of a group of cells, could do a better job of carrying out the functions of the body.

Corals. These tiny soft-bodied animals contain a hard, lime-like substance which they secrete from their bodies, building strong supports around them. Hordes of corals crowd together and become joined into great coral reefs hundreds of miles long. They even build entire islands. In Cambrian times, the first supports

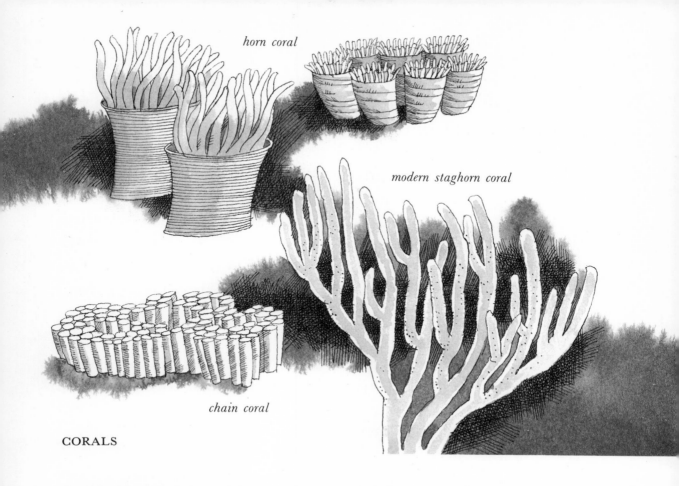

horn coral

modern staghorn coral

chain coral

CORALS

built by corals were small cones with ridges to which the coral bodies fastened themselves. As millions of years passed, the shapes changed. Some assumed various horn shapes.

Corals today appear in many odd and beautiful shapes.

Jellyfish. Impressions of jellyfish left in Cambrian and Pre-Cambrian rocks show them to have been similar to our modern species which drifts or swims in seas all over the world today. The jellyfish has a round mouth with tentacles hanging from it. These tentacles have stinging cells. The jellyfish stings small sea creatures and eats them. It has a hollow cavity inside its body which acts as a stomach. Although jellyfish are soft-bodied, many of them were preserved because they were washed onto beaches, where their bodies dried out, became covered with sand, and left imprints in the mud which hardened into rock. These imprinted rocks became fossils.

Sea Anemones. Fossil remains of these animals, which are closely related to jellyfish, are rare. Since most sea

JELLYFISH

SEA ANEMONE

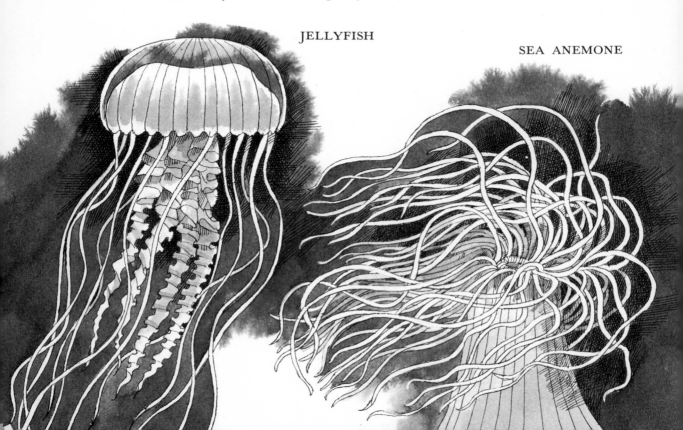

anemones were attached to a stone as they grew, they probably did not get tossed up on shore so frequently as the drifting jellyfish did. Nevertheless, scientists believe they existed in Cambrian times. The sea anemone looks like an upside-down jellyfish. Its waving tentacles, which make it look like a beautiful flower, are filled with a poison that can kill small fishes and other sea animals.

PLATYHELMINTHES
the first animals with a brain

The PLATYHELMINTHES (PLATT-ee-hel-MIN-theez), a family of flatworms, include tapeworms, flukes, and other worm-like creatures which are sometimes found feeding in the intestines of men or animals.

The flatworm was the first animal to develop a real head with nerve tissue forming a brain and a system of nerve cells that could carry a signal from the brain to any part of the body. It was also the first animal to evolve muscle-building cells. These show the flatworm to have been advanced in the evolutionary pattern of life. Fossils of flatworms are rare, but some

23

ANNELID

PLATYHELMINTH

of the burrows and trails that have been found in Pre-Cambrian and Cambrian rocks may have been made by them.

ANNELIDS
segmented worms

Another group of worms is the ANNELIDS (AN-nell-ids), which includes earthworms or angleworms. The bodies of these worms consist of many sections strung together like beads. Their ancestors probably crawled about the muddy sea bottom searching for food. Trails, burrows, and castings of their wastes have been found in Cambrian rocks.

24

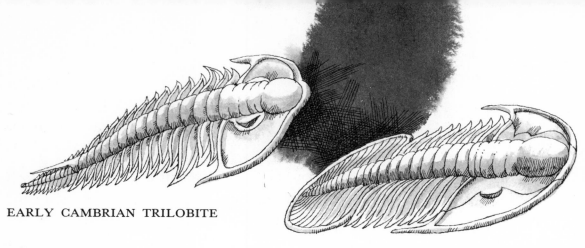

EARLY CAMBRIAN TRILOBITE

MIDDLE CAMBRIAN TRILOBITE

TRILOBITES
rulers of the Cambrian seas

Trilobites were so named because their bodies are divided lengthwise into three parts, or "lobes." The large number of fossils appearing in Cambrian rocks show that the seas at this time were teeming with trilobites. They swam or crawled about on the sea bottom, snapping up the soft-bodied creatures all around them.

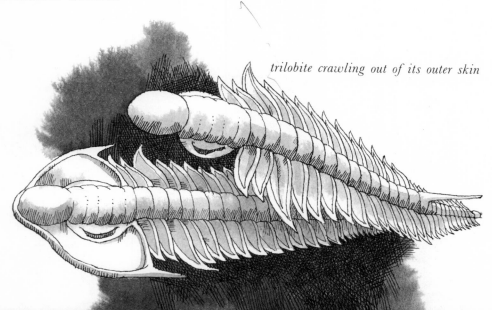

trilobite crawling out of its outer skin

Trilobites belong to a group which is known as ARTHROPODS (AR-throe-PODS), or "jointed legs." This includes crabs, shrimps, lobsters, spiders, scorpions, centipedes, and others. Trilobites had a tough, crusty outer skin which, although not hard enough to be called a shell, protected the body like armor. As a trilobite grew, it shed its outer skin, and then grew a new skin to fit its larger body. It may have done this several times during its lifetime.

While some trilobites were small—less than one inch long—over millions of years some grew to be more than two feet long. They ruled the seas for almost a hundred million years, then became scarcer and scarcer. Finally they became extinct. No one knows exactly why, but one of the reasons may have been the rise of a group of fierce meat-eaters—ancestors of our octopuses—who probably preyed on them.

HORSESHOE CRABS
ancient and modern

The earliest horseshoe crabs lived as early as the

CAMBRIAN HORSESHOE CRAB

about 4 inches long

MODERN HORSESHOE CRAB

almost 2 feet long

Cambrian Period, about five hundred million years ago. These ancient species looked more like trilobites, with a body consisting of eleven sections. Over many millions of years, their descendants went through many changes, until during the Permian Period the horseshoe crab evolved with a body resembling its present form—two sections with a long spike tail. The first of these true horseshoe crabs were tiny—some not more than one inch long. But they grew larger and larger. Today some are nearly two feet long. You might see one on a sandy shore anywhere along the Atlantic Ocean from Canada to the Gulf of Mexico.

The Ordovician Period

515 to 460 million years ago

The end of a period and the beginning of a new one may be marked by the extinction of certain species of living things and the appearance of others. During the almost 100 million years of the Cambrian Period, which preceded the Ordovician, the surface of the earth had changed many times. At times the seas drained off as the lands rose. At other times the seas overflowed the lands.

28

During Ordovician times, more than half of North America was covered with shallow seas. These seas were swarming with invertebrates, animals without backbones. Although many were similar to the creatures which had existed in Cambrian times, most were new species which had developed hard, thick shells. These shells were more likely to be preserved as fossils than were the softer-shelled Cambrian creatures. On the other hand, there were still some clams with shells that were too thin to become complete fossils. These merely left molds of their shells imprinted in Ordovician rocks.

MOLLUSKS

The name MOLLUSKS (MOLL-usks) means "soft ones," for most mollusks have soft bodies covered by shells. The Ordovician seas were teeming with many kinds of mollusks which scientists have classified in the following three groups:

29

Pelecypods (pe-LESS-i-podz), "hatchet feet," include a wide variety of clams, oysters, mussels, and similar creatures having shells with two equal parts called "valves." The shells are fastened together with a hinge-like closing. Inside the shell there is a soft body with no head. The feet are usually shaped like the blade of a hatchet. Although Ordovician times are noted for animals with hard, thick shells, the clams at this time still had thin shells which were not strong enough to last through millions of years in order to become fossils. Therefore, most of the clam fossils are mere impressions of shells which were left to harden in mud or sand. Some impressions show the shape of the outside of the shell, others the inside, so that we have an indication of how the muscles were attached to the shell.

After many millions of years passed, clams built thicker and stronger shells. These, along with shells of oysters and mussels, are found preserved whole in rocks of much later periods.

Gastropods (GAS-tro-PODZ), "stomach feet," constitute a wide variety of snails, limpets, and other creatures which crawl on their flat undersides. The snails of the Ordovician Period lived in the seas. They had thick shells coiled into a variety of shapes and they snuggled their bodies into the largest coil. In some ways they were very much like today's snails.

When a snail becomes frightened, it pulls back into its shell. Some snails have a little door on the back which is called an *operculum* (o-PUR-kyu-lum). The snail can close this door after himself and feel safe when he is being pursued. Some snails of Ordovician times had operculums, and it is assumed that their habits were like those of similar snails today.

Snails in many shapes and forms lived on through all of the Paleozoic Era, through the more than two

SNAIL

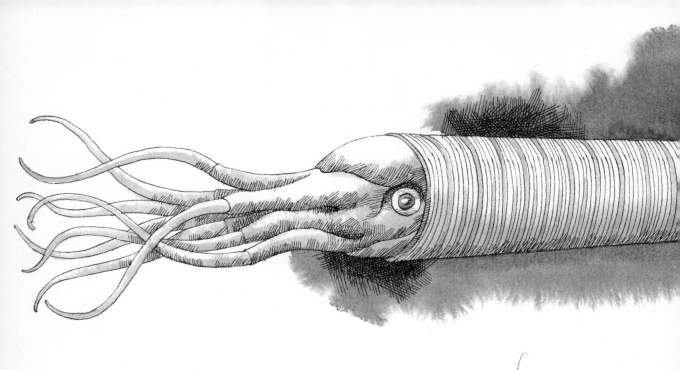

hundred million years which followed, and into the present. Ancient shells have been found in many fossil beds in North America and in other places in the world. Some of today's snails live in water, as their ancestors did; others live on land. Some snails can swim, others can crawl, and some can do both.

Cephalopods (SEF-a-lo-PODZ), "head feet," make up the third group of ancient mollusks. They were fierce monsters of the Ordovician seas, related to today's squids and octopuses. Some, like the octopus, had no body coverings. But a large number built tough shells

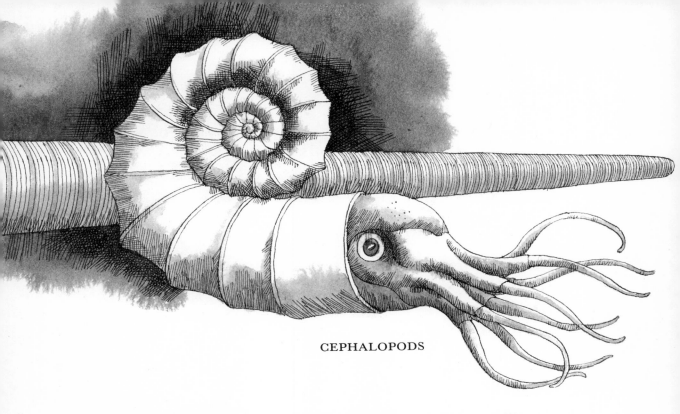

CEPHALOPODS

around themselves and are referred to as "horn shells." Some of the shells were straight or cone-shaped; others were tightly coiled like a snail's shell.

The cephalopods were the most advanced of the mollusks. They had nerves in the head that probably acted as a brain, two large eyes, and a mouth surrounded by tentacles or "arms." The horn shell's head was at the hind part of the shell where one might expect the feet to be, hence the name "head feet." It could stretch out its "arms" to gather food, or it could use them as feet to walk around on the sea bottom. In order to walk with its "arms" it had to get into an upright position with its head downward. Many cephalopods also swam in the water like squids.

While some cephalopods were only a few inches long, some of the straight-shelled ones grew as large as ten to fifteen feet long. They preyed on many kinds of sea animals.

Horn shells lived on in various forms for almost three hundred million years, throughout the rest of the Paleozoic Era. Some have lived on into modern times. Fossils have been found in North America as well as in Europe and other parts of the world.

BRACHIOPODS
rulers of the Ordovician seas

A BRACHIOPOD (BRAK-ee-o-POD) looks somewhat like a clam, but it differs in both the inner body and the shell. Instead of having two matching shells, the top shell of one kind of brachiopod is rounded and the bottom shell is curved in a horn-like shape. When the top shell is cut away, the bottom shell reminds one of an ancient oil lamp. Therefore, these brachiopods are often called "lamp shells."

34

Brachiopods had existed long before Ordovician times, but they were small and thin shelled. In the Ordovician Period, the brachiopods developed hard, thick, stony shells. There were hundreds of species, and they became the rulers of the seas. Some had short stalks which they attached to rocks or other shells; others had long stalks which they buried in sand or soft mud; still others either had no stalks to begin with or had lost them.

A modern version of the long-stalked variety of brachiopod is called *lingula* (LING-goo-la). It has a thick, twisting stalk with which it digs into the sand of shallow sea bottoms. The lingula is found today around the Philippine islands.

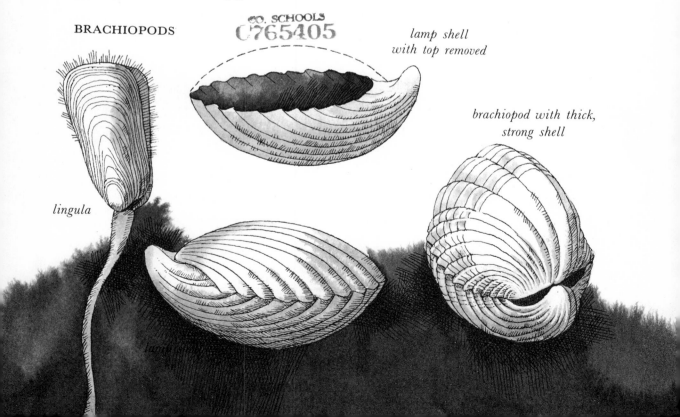

BRACHIOPODS

lamp shell with top removed

brachiopod with thick, strong shell

lingula

Brachiopods were numerous all through the Paleozoic Era but became rare after that time. In modern times, there are only a little more than a hundred species of brachiopods, compared to about ten thousand kinds of clams.

The Silurian Period

460 to 405 million years ago

Europe was mostly dry and mountainous during the Silurian Period, but most of North America was covered by seas at various times, and sea life was bountiful. During this time, some of the primitive sea plants which had been washed ashore began to grow on land. These were mostly moss-like plants without leaves, stem, or root, thriving on damp ground.

Of the sea creatures, trilobites, brachiopods, and mollusks of all types were present in great numbers. Another group, including starfish, sea urchins, and sand dollars, made an appearance. And most important of all, during the Silurian Period there was an abundance of primitive fishes, namely the group of OSTRACODERMS (aw-STRAK-o-durmz), which are known as "armored fishes." The ostracoderms were the earliest form of VERTEBRATES (VER-te-brates), animals with backbones. The *true* vertebrates evolved millions of years later, in the Devonian Period.

ECHINODERMS
"spiny skins"

The group of invertebrates which is known as ECHINODERMS (ee-KY-no-durmz) includes starfish, sea urchins, sand dollars, and flower-like animals growing on stalks. As their nickname "spiny skins" implies, they are covered with sharp spines or stony plates. Echinoderms existed in both Cambrian and Ordovician times, but became particularly prominent in the Silurian Period. The most important of the flower-like animals on stalks were called *crinoids*. They were present in Silurian times in large numbers, but became even more abundant in the Carboniferous Period.

Starfish. Is it a fish? No, it is one of the echinoderms. No one knows exactly when or why it was named a star*fish*, except that many centuries ago almost any animal that came out of the sea was referred to as a fish. The earliest starfish was apparently shaped like a flattened ball. But this creature later evolved with five arms reaching out in the shape of a star, as it appears today. Each of these arms contains a branch of the stomach and other organs. Long tubes at the tip of each point feel for food and bring it to the mouth, which is at the center of the underpart of the body.

Fossils of starfish are rare, but some have been found attached to the shells of clams on which they may have been feeding when they became buried together in mud or sand. Other starfish fossils have been found as imprints in rocks.

Sea Urchins and Sand Dollars. These members of the group of echinoderms are covered with round, oval,

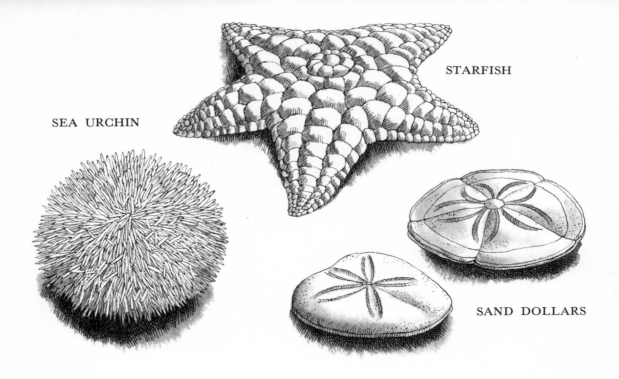

SEA URCHIN

STARFISH

SAND DOLLARS

or heart-shaped plates. Some sea urchins wear a thick coat of spines.

OSTRACODERMS
"bony skins"

In the Silurian Period, OSTRACODERMS, strange fish-like creatures, swam in shallow seas. They were small, and their heads and bodies were covered with bony plates. Often referred to as "armored fishes," they were the earliest vertebrates.

40

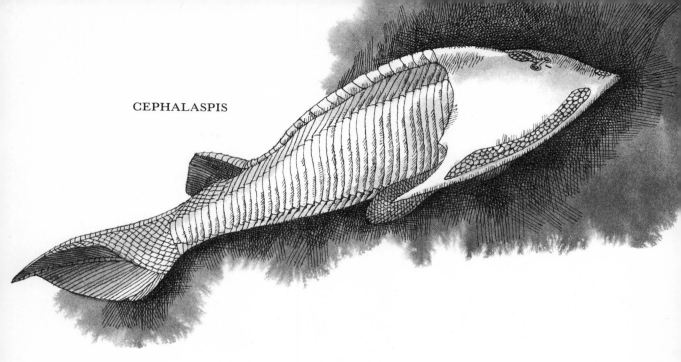

CEPHALASPIS

The ostracoderms were shaped like fishes and had tails, but they did not have fins growing in pairs as modern fishes do. Instead of jaws which could be opened for biting, they had only a slit for a mouth opening. Therefore they are sometimes called "jawless." Having no jaws, they were probably obliged to subsist on only the soft food to be found in the mud at the bottom of the sea. Many ostracoderms became extinct in the Silurian Period, but some lived on into the early part of the Devonian Period. Later these also became extinct.

Cephalaspis (sef-a-LAS-pis) is one of the best known ostracoderms. His head was covered with a shield of

41

bony plate and his tail was covered with movable bony plates. Under the helmet-like headshield was a skull with eyes, brain, and nerves. There was a fin on his back and another on the end of his tail. Like other ostracoderms he was jawless, having only a slit for a mouth. Cephalaspis was only seven inches long, but some ostracoderms were even smaller, while others were as long as a foot or more.

EURYPTERIDS
"sea scorpions"

As previously noted, many of the ostracoderms became extinct in the late Silurian and early Devonian Periods. What was the cause of their disappearance? Some scientists think the EURYPTERIDS (yoo-RIP-te-ridz), or sea scorpions, fierce creatures with powerful biting mouths, preyed on these armored fishes and were able to bite through their bony plates and kill them for food. While some sea scorpions were no more than five inches long, others grew to become the largest invertebrates living in shallow seas. (The larger octopus-like creatures

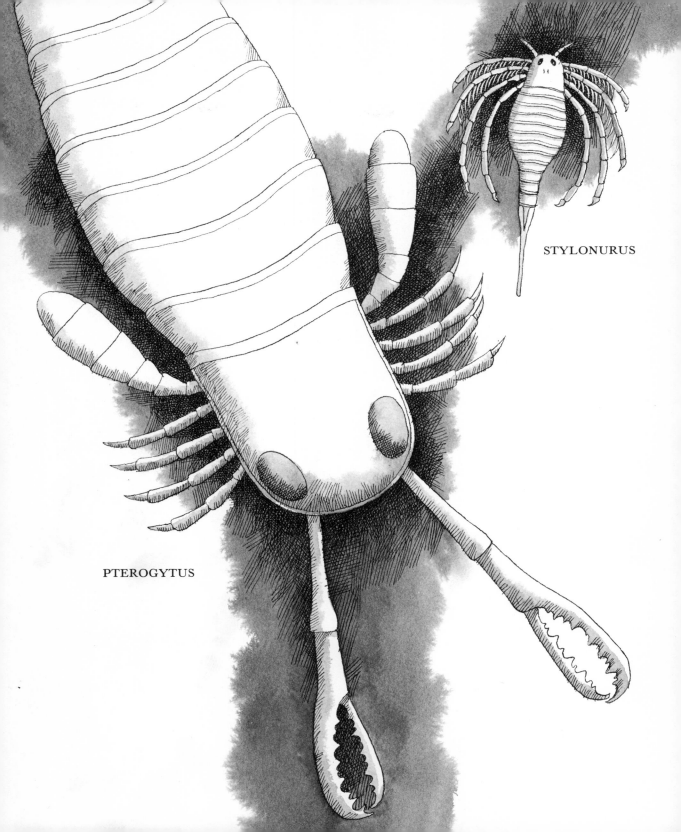

STYLONURUS

PTEROGYTUS

which were also in existence at that time lived far out in the oceans.)

Pterogytus (ter-o-GIE-tus) was the largest of all sea scorpions (about eight to ten feet long). Sea scorpions belong to the arthropods. Like other members of this group, Pterogytus had a jointed body with jointed legs, two of which had become thick and acted as paddles to help him swim. At his head, he had sawtoothed claws which he used for catching food and for fighting.

Stylonurus (sty-LON-er-us) was a comparatively small sea scorpion—only about five inches long—but equally dangerous to smaller sea animals. He had a jointed body and ten jointed legs, but did not have the two claw-like pincers of his huge relative Pterogytus. On the end of his tail, Stylonurus had a sharp spike.

The Devonian Period

405 to 345 million years ago

The Devonian Period is often referred to as the "Age of Fishes." Large portions of North America were at various times covered with water. Almost all the sea creatures of previous periods had survived in various species. The seas were full of sponges, snails, corals,

45

brachiopods, echinoderms, huge trilobites about two feet long, and many other invertebrates.

In Devonian times, primitive plants and animals from the seas took up life on land. The plants were mostly the moss-like types which must have begun living at a much earlier period. Once the plants had established themselves on land, animals appeared which fed on the plants or smaller animals. Among them were land scorpions, spiders, and small wingless insects.

Now, the greatest drama of the seas took place—the rise of the *true fishes,* animals with backbones similar to those of today's vertebrates. Most important of all, some fishes developed lungs for breathing air and were able to crawl out onto land, eventually evolving into AMPHIBIANS (am-FIB-ians), animals which live both on land and in water.

PLACODERMS
"plated skins"

PLACODERMS (PLAK-o-durmz) had shields of armor covering the head and parts of the body, as did earlier primitive fish-like animals, but they had some new

46

features which identify them as *one of the first groups of true fishes.* Instead of just a slit for a mouth, the placoderm had bony jaws which he could open wide for biting. Also, he had a long streamlined body and a pair of fins to help him swim. Now, instead of grubbing in the mud for food, he could chase after smaller fishes.

Dinichthys (din-IK-this), "terrible fish," also known as *Dunkleosteus* (DUNKLE-os-tus), was about thirty feet long and was the cannibal of Devonian seas. He had tremendous biting jaws which could crush his victim with one snap. Fossils of this giant fish have been found in Ohio, where a sea once covered the state.

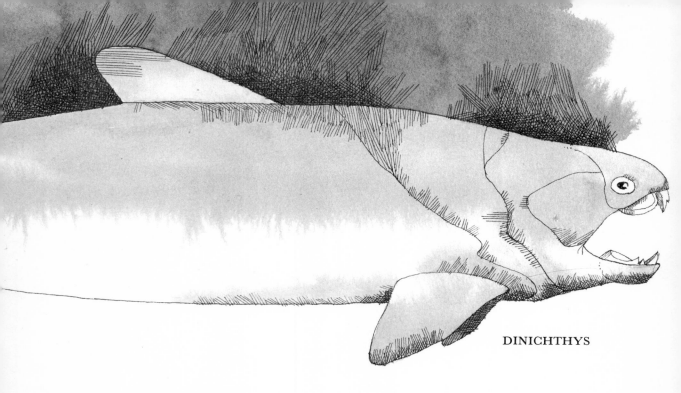

DINICHTHYS

CHONDRICTHYES

Toward the end of the Devonian Period, a different group of fishes known as CHONDRICTHYES (kahn-DRIK-thi-eez) developed. Instead of their skeletons being made of true bone, they were made of a substance called cartilage. This kind of cartilage differs in content from true bone, but it may be just as hard. It differs also from the softer cartilage we have in our noses, ears, and some other parts of our bodies.

These cartilage fishes were sharks. They were of many different sizes, from about four to twelve or

49

CLADOSELACHE

MODERN BLUE SHARK

MODERN TIGER SHARK

more feet long. As millions of years went by, at least one species of sharks became tremendous in size—as long as fifty feet, with giant-size jaws equipped with hard dagger-like teeth.

Descendants of the early sharks survive today in many different species. There are changes in the details of their bodies, but their skeletons are similar.

Cladoselache (klad-o-SELL-ah-kee), one of the early sharks, was about four feet long. The fins suggest that he lived in the open seas.

OSTEICHTHYES
"bony fishes"

At about the same time that the "cartilage fishes" were developing, another group, destined to become the most successful of all fishes, was evolving as well. These were the OSTEICHTHYES (AW-stee-IK-thi-eez), "bony fishes," with skeletons built of hard, strong bones. In the early part of the Devonian Period, the bodies of these fishes were completely covered with bony scales, and their heads and shoulders were cov-

51

ered with bony plates. As millions of years went by, most of their descendants lost the head coverings, but they retained the bony skeletons that have survived to this day in most of our modern fishes.

Climatus (kly-MAY-tus) was one of the ancestors of today's bony fishes. He was tiny—only about three inches long. Instead of having the usual two pairs of fins found on present-day fishes, he had many separate pairs of fins. Each fin carried a bony spike. He also had scales on his body, as the later bony fishes do.

CLIMATUS

CROSSOPTERYGIANS

During the Devonian Period, some fishes developed lungs for breathing on land. This was a great advantage. During dry periods, when many fishes were unable to survive, a lungfish could hide itself below the surface of the mud, leaving only a small hole for breathing, and thus exist for many months until the rains returned.

Foremost among the lungfish was a special group called CROSSOPTERYGIANS (kross-AHP-te-RIJ-i-unz), or "fringe fins." In addition to lungs, a fish of this group had a backbone, a brain, and sturdy side-fins called "lobes" which were edged with a fringe-like border of thin bones connected by skin. These lobes contained muscles and bones that could eventually evolve into the legs and feet of a more advanced animal. When the pools of water dried up, a fringe fin could crawl out on land and creep along on its lobes in search of other waters. Over millions of years, improvements in offspring produced new kinds of animals which were able to live part of the time on land and part of the time in water. These are called AMPHIBIANS, meaning "living both." Today's am-

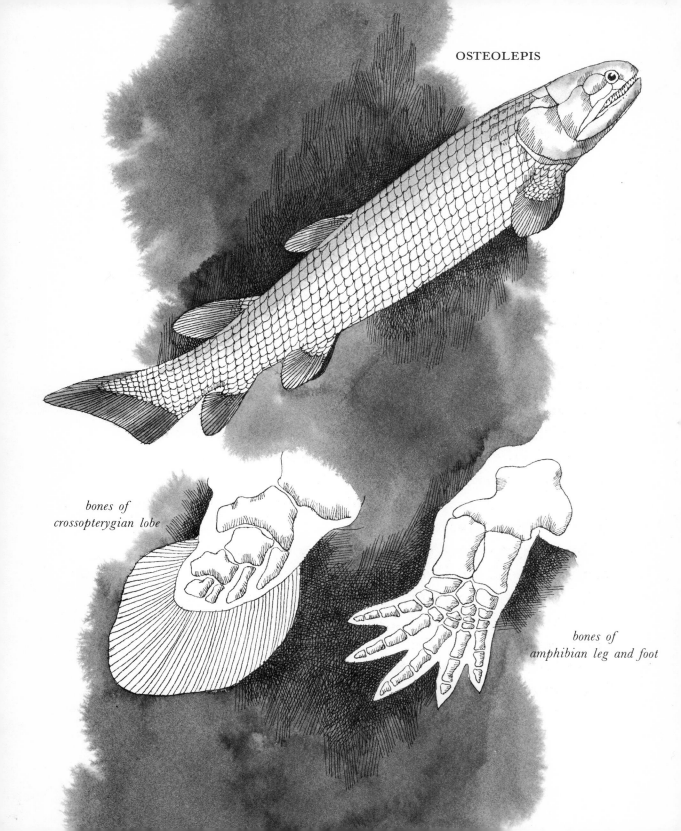

OSTEOLEPIS

bones of
crossopterygian lobe

bones of
amphibian leg and foot

phibians are frogs, toads, newts, and salamanders.

Osteolepis (os-tee-o-LEEP-is), a "fringe fin," was one of the early lungfish which crawled out on land in Devonian times. He was about nine inches long.

RISE OF THE AMPHIBIANS

In the latter part of the Devonian Period, amphibians which had evolved from fringe-fin lungfish appeared in great numbers and varieties in the swamps and surrounding deltas.

An amphibian spends most of its time on land but must return to water to lay its jelly-like eggs, which do not have a hard protective shell. At first, the baby amphibians breathe through gills, as a fish does, so they have to remain in water until their lungs have developed for breathing. Then they are ready to make their own way on land.

Some of the primitive amphibians resembled salamanders, with long, slender bodies. Others were more

55

like lizards, snakes, or crocodiles. Some were small, with bodies covered with fine scales. Larger ones were covered with heavy armor-like bony plates.

Ichthyostega (IK-thi-o-STEE-ga), an early amphibian, lived in lakes and rivers in what is now the country of Greenland. He was four feet long, with a body resembling a salamander. He had legs and feet for crawling.

ICHTHYOSTEGA

The Carboniferous Period

Mississippian Period—355 to 345 million years ago

Pennsylvanian Period—330 to 265 million years ago

The Carboniferous Period was a time of giant forests with a lush growth of primitive plants. Whenever the seas receded, they left much swampy land which, together with a mild, humid climate, created a perfect atmosphere for plant life.

Primitive *scale trees* grew to heights of sixty to one hundred feet. These trees had slim leaves growing directly out from the trunks and branches. When the leaves fell off, they left marks resembling scales; thus, the name.

Tree ferns, also giants of their kind, grew up to fifty feet tall. (Some tree ferns exist in tropical climates today.) Horsetails, which today are only a few feet tall, reached heights of thirty feet.

Every so often, during the many millions of years of Carboniferous times, the seas overflowed the land, burying the forests. When the seas drained off again, new forests grew over the buried ones. And over millions of years, the dead plant material in the ground became compressed and formed coal. The Carboniferous Period has therefore been called the "Coal Age."

Many kinds of creatures made their homes in the Carboniferous forests—cockroaches, spiders, land scorpions, and enormous dragonflies with wings that extended to thirty inches in flight. And on the edges of the swamps, amphibians multiplied in many varieties.

AMPHIBIANS EVOLVE INTO REPTILES

Over millions of years, amphibians developed body structures that helped them to move faster and to get along better on land.

In the Pennsylvanian part of the Carboniferous Period, a great step forward in evolution took place: the development of land eggs. Instead of being soft and jelly-like, they had a hard outer shell. They were laid on land rather than in the water, and were left for the sun to hatch. The inside of the egg had a yolk (as a chicken egg does today). The yolk supplied food to the unborn babies, and around the yolk were the watery surroundings which the offspring needed in order to develop. Most important of all, now for the first time, the babies were *born with lungs* for breathing on land. Thus, unlike amphibians, which are hatched in water and must live there until the lungs develop, these babies were able to get along on land immediately after birth. These creatures were not amphibians, but REPTILES, which had been evolving over millions of years.

While reptiles lived very successfully on land during the Permian Period, some spent part of their time in water, just as some do today. Today's reptiles are

DIPLOVERTEBRON

crocodiles, turtles, lizards, snakes, and the small rare tuatara.

Diplovertebron (dip-lo-VER-te-bron) was a typical emerging reptile, combining the characteristics of amphibians and reptiles. He was about four inches long. His remains were found in Bohemia, which is now Czechoslovakia.

60

LIFE IN CARBONIFEROUS SEAS

When seas overflowed the lands in Carboniferous times, many creatures learned to live in the waters. Among the strangest were torpedo-shaped mollusks resembling the horn shells.

Belemnoids (BEL-em-noyds), of the cephalopod family, first appeared in the early part of the Carboniferous Period and lived in increasing numbers for about two hundred million years. They became extinct, however, about sixty million years ago.

Unlike the horn shell, which built a shell around itself, the belemnoid had a cone-shaped shell *inside* the front part of its body and two fins spreading sideways

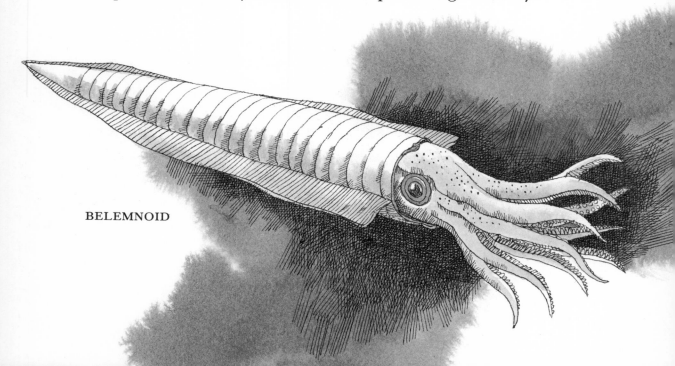

BELEMNOID

which helped it to balance itself. The head had two large round eyes and ten arms extending from its mouth. As the creature darted backward or forward in jet-like spurts, the arms could gather small fish and bring them to the mouth for feeding.

Like the modern squid, which is believed to be a possible descendant, the belemnoid carried inside its body a sac of inky liquid which it could shoot out for protection as it swam away from an enemy.

Crinoids (CRY-noidz)—"sea lilies." Is it a flower? No. It's a sea animal related to the starfish and sea urchin. All are members of the echinoderm family. Some sea lilies drifted in large clusters on the seas, but most lived on the bottom and built stiff, jointed stalks ending in roots which clung tightly to the mud or sand. The body of the animal, shaped somewhat like a lily, formed the flower-like top. The animal was covered with plates and had many arms which waved in the water, gathering food and bringing it to the mouth at the very top of the "flower." Crinoids began in Ordovician seas or even earlier, but they increased in great numbers and varieties during Silurian and Carboniferous times, and some continue to exist. About eight hundred species live today in very deep waters.

CRINOIDS

The Permian Period

265 to 225 million years ago

Again the earth's surface and climate changed. In a
large part of North America, many of the seas grew
shallow and disappeared during Permian times.
Mountains rose in Europe, Asia, and the eastern part
of North America. Glaciers covered many parts of the

64

world. Therefore the climate became colder and drier. Most of the swamps dried up and the coal forests could no longer thrive. A new kind of trees similar to today's spruces and pines formed new forests.

The Permian forests were teeming with insect life. Ancestors of the stonefly, mayfly, grasshopper, roach, and earwig, among others, have been found as Permian fossils.

Although most of the land was dry, the seas had not disappeared entirely, and a wide variety of creatures existed in them, including some land animals which returned to the sea.

In some areas, especially in northern Texas, some swamps still existed. Certain amphibians became very large and important in the swampland. Eventually, many strange reptiles took over the land. Some of these reptiles had mammal-like characteristics, although mammals did not evolve until many millions of years later.

ERYOPS

CACOPS

DIPLOCAULUS

AMPHIBIANS OF THE PERMIAN PERIOD

Eryops (ER-ee-ops) was a more advanced amphibian than the primitive Ichthyostega of the Devonian Period. Eryops lived two hundred and fifty million years ago in northern Texas, which was mostly swampland at that time. He was huge for an amphibian, about six to seven feet long, with large tooth-filled jaws. He lived near the shore and probably crawled out onto the banks to sun himself. Specimens have been found not only in Texas, but in other parts of North America and also in Europe.

Cacops (KAY-kops) was one of a group of small amphibians which crawled on land in Permian times. He was only sixteen inches long but had a large head and jaws. A stiff ridge of bone along his spine may have protected him from his enemies, so that he became one of the most successful of the small amphibians living on land.

Diplocaulus (DIP-lo-CAWL-us) also lived in Texas during Permian times. This strange amphibian had a wide triangular head made of hard bone, with his mouth on the underside. He had short, weak legs which were not much use for crawling on land, so he apparently lay at the bottom of streams or swamps grubbing for food.

MESOSAURUS

SEA REPTILES OF PERMIAN TIMES

During the Permian Period, some reptiles which had lived on land returned to living in water. While they lived and swam like fishes, they had four limbs and finger-like parts which show they were not fishes, but reptiles.

68

Mesosaurus (mess-o-SAWR-us), a fierce-looking sea reptile, was only about twenty-eight inches long, but his long jaws with their many fine, sharp teeth probably made a quick meal of any smaller water creature. Remains have been found in South Africa and Brazil.

MAMMAL-LIKE REPTILES

In the latter part of the Permian Period, some very strange-looking reptiles lived on the dry lands which rose among the swamps of Texas. Some of these reptiles had mammal-like teeth. Some were plant-eaters. But wherever there are plant-eaters, there are usually meat-eaters who prey on them.

Dimetrodon (di-MET-ro-don), a large mammal-like reptile, was a ferocious meat-eater about eleven feet long, weighing more than 600 pounds. His name refers to two lengths of teeth—long, dagger-like stabbers at the front of the mouth and short cutting teeth at the sides. On his back he carried a tall sail which grew as high as four feet.

There are several theories among scientists as to the

purpose of the sail. Some think it absorbed heat from the sun in cold weather and radiated heat outward to keep the animal cool in hot weather. This would be useful to a reptile, because reptiles cannot control their temperatures internally. If the weather is too

DIMETRODON

cold, a reptile slows down until it is hardly able to move. If the weather is too warm, the reptile must seek shade.

Other scientists think the sail helped Dimetrodon to hide among the jungle foliage until his prey approached, making it easier for him to attack.

Edaphosaurus (e-DAF-o-sawr-us) was one of the mammal-like reptiles. Judging by his blunt teeth, he was a plant-eater. But he also probably ate clams and

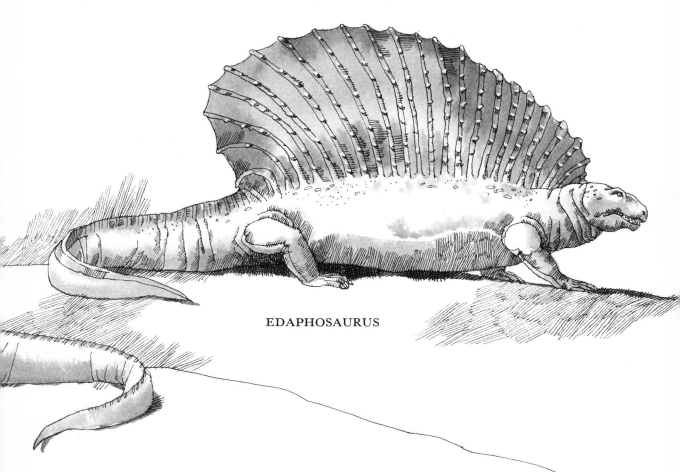

EDAPHOSAURUS

snails. On his back he carried a sail consisting of short, thick spines covered with a web of skin. No one really knows what the purpose of the sail was, but some think it was a device to control his own temperature. Edaphosaurus weighed about 350 to 600 pounds.

Moschops (MOSS-kops) was a strange mammal-like animal more than seven feet long which lived on the banks of desert rivers in South Africa during Permian times. Some scientists say that he showed features of both reptiles and mammals. (Mammals did not appear until many millions of years later.)

MOSCHOPS

End of the Paleozoic Era

The Permian Period marked the end of the Paleozoic Era, the millions of years in which so many fascinating creatures lived BEFORE THE DINOSAURS.

By the time the Permian Period ended, dramatic changes had taken place on earth. Many groups of plants and animals had become extinct. But many reptiles continued to swarm over the earth.

One group of reptiles, known as ROMERIIDS (RO-mer-EE-yidz), was very significant to the pattern of living things to come in the new eras which followed. The romeriids are said to be the ancestors of five branches of animal life—turtles, mammals, fish reptiles, sea serpents, and THECODONTS (THEE-co-donts)—which were in turn the ancestors of dinosaurs, as well as crocodiles, birds, flying reptiles, tuataras, lizards, and snakes.

74

HYLONOMUS

Hylonomus (HY-lo-NO-mus), a typical early reptile or romeriid, has been found in Nova Scotia. He was not very large—only about eight inches long—but he is considered a link between amphibians, reptiles, and mammals. He is especially notable as an evolutionary ancestor of the dinosaur.

VISIT YOUR LOCAL MUSEUM

After reading about fossils, it's fun to see them. Almost every state in the union has one or more museums where fossil collections can be seen. These are some of the museums which have good collections of fossils of animals and plants that lived BEFORE THE DINOSAURS:

American Museum of Natural History, New York City

Smithsonian Institution, Washington, D. C.

Chicago Natural History Museum, Chicago, Illinois

Cleveland Museum of Natural History, Cleveland, Ohio

County Museum of Natural History, Los Angeles, California

National Museum of Canada, Ottawa, Canada

Carnegie Museum, Pittsburgh, Pennsylvania

Exhibit Museum, University of Michigan, Ann Arbor, Michigan

If none of the museums listed is near you, ask your teacher or librarian to help you find a museum in your locality.

BOOKS ABOUT PREHISTORIC LIFE
for Young Readers

TALES TOLD BY FOSSILS *by Carroll Lane Fenton*
> Doubleday & Company, Inc., Garden City, New York, 1966

THE STORY OF LIFE *by Peter Farb*
> Harvey House, Irvington-on-Hudson, New York, 1962

IN PREHISTORIC SEAS *by Carroll L. Fenton and Mildred A. Fenton*
> John Day Company, New York, 1962

THE WONDERS OF LIFE ON EARTH *by the editors of* Life *and Lincoln Barnett* (specially adapted by Sarel Eimerl)
> Golden Press, New York, 1960

HOW TO KNOW DINOSAURS *by Carla Greene*
> The Bobbs-Merrill Company, Inc., New York, 1966

AFTER THE DINOSAURS *by Carla Greene*
> The Bobbs-Merrill Company, Inc., New York, 1968

CHARLES DARWIN *by Carla Greene*
> The Dial Press, Inc., New York, 1968

GREGOR MENDEL *by Carla Greene*
> The Dial Press, Inc., New York, 1970

THE WONDERFUL WORLD OF LIFE *by Julian Huxley*
> Garden City Books, Garden City, New York, 1958

MORE ADVANCED BOOKS

EVOLUTION IN ACTION *by Julian Huxley*
New American Library, New York, 1957

THE FOSSIL BOOK *by Carroll L. Fenton and Mildred A. Fenton*
Doubleday & Company, Inc., Garden City, New York, 1958

ILLUSTRATED GUIDE TO FOSSIL COLLECTING *by Richard Casanova*
Naturegraph, San Mateo, California, 1957

LIFE OF THE PAST *by George G. Simpson*
Yale University Press, New Haven, Conn., 1953

MAN, TIME AND FOSSILS *by Ruth Moore*
Knopf Publishing, New York, 1953

VERTEBRATE PALEONTOLOGY *by Alfred S. Romer*
University of Chicago Press, Chicago, Illinois, 1966
(Supplement, 1968)

Index